Tyrannosaurus Rex

by Daniel Cohen

Consultant:
Brent Breithaupt,
Director
Geological Museum
University of Wyoming

Bridgestone Books
an imprint of Capstone Press
Mankato, Minnesota

Bridgestone Books are published by Capstone Press
151 Good Counsel Drive, P.O. Box 669, Mankato, Minnesota 56002
http://www.capstonepress.com

Library of Congress Cataloging-in-Publication Data
Cohen, Daniel, 1936–
    Tyrannosaurus rex/by Daniel Cohen.
    p. cm.—(The Bridgestone Science Library)
    Includes bibliographical references and index.
    Summary: Discusses the physical characteristics, habitat, food, defenses, relatives,
and extinction of the largest meat-eating dinosaur.
    ISBN 0-7368-3462-1 (paperback) ISBN 0-7368-0620-2 (hardcover)
    1. Tyrannosaurus rex—Juvenile literature. [1. Tyrannosaurus rex. 2. The Bridgestone
Science Library.] I. Title. II. Series
QE862.S3 C565 2001
567.912'9—dc21   00-021736

Editorial Credits

Erika Mikkelson, editor; Linda Clavel, cover designer and illustrator; Heidi Schoof
    and Kimberly Danger, photo researchers

Photo Credits

American Museum of Natural History, 10–11
Diane Meyer, cover, 1
Francois Gohier, 16, 20
Gary Neal Corbett, 4–5, 8
Thomas Kitchin/TOM STACK & ASSOCIATES, 14
Visuals Unlimited/Ken Lucas, 6; Mark E. Gibson, 12–13

1 2 3 4 5 6 08 07 06 05 04 03

Table of Contents

Tyrannosaurus Rex

The name Tyrannosaurus rex (ty-RAN-oh-SORE-us REX) means king tyrant reptile. Tyrannosaurus rex was one of the largest meat-eating dinosaurs. It measured 46 feet (14 meters) long from nose to tail. It stood 18 feet (5 meters) tall and weighed 8 tons (7 metric tons).

tyrant
something that rules over others in a mean way

The World of Tyrannosaurus Rex

Tyrannosaurus rex lived 70 million to 65 million years ago. The dinosaur lived in what is now the western United States and Canada. The climate was warm and wet during the time Tyrannosaurus rex lived.

climate
the usual weather in a place

This dinosaur is Albertosaurus.
Tyrannosaurus rex and
Albertosaurus were tyrannosaurids.

Tyrannosaurus Rex

Tyrannosaurus rex was a tyrannosaurid (ty-RAN-oh-SORE-id). This group of meat-eating dinosaurs walked on their two back legs. Tyrannosaurids had tiny arms with two fingers. Tyrannosaurus rex was one of the largest tyrannosaurids.

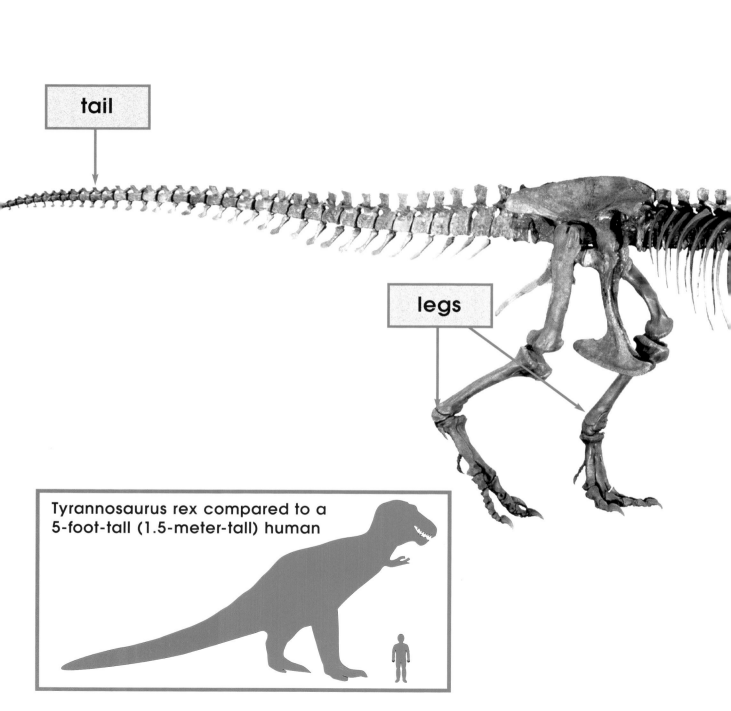

tail

legs

Tyrannosaurus rex compared to a
5-foot-tall (1.5-meter-tall) human

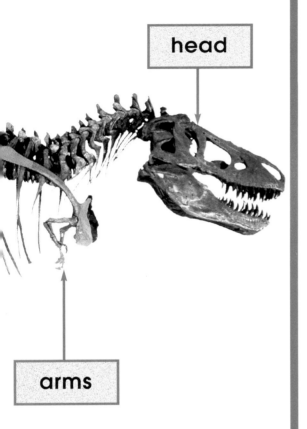

head

arms

Parts of Tyrannosaurus Rex

Tyrannosaurus rex walked and ran on two large, powerful back legs. Its two tiny arms had two fingers on each hand. The dinosaur's large head measured 5 feet (1.5 meters) long. Sharp teeth filled the dinosaur's mouth. A thick tail helped to balance its heavy head.

...us Rex Ate

...was a

...ur. Some

scientists believe it attacked plant-eating dinosaurs such as Triceratops (try-SERR-a-tops). Tyrannosaurus rex wandered the plains where its prey lived.

prey
an animal that is hunted by another animal for food

13

Hunting

Tyrannosaurus rex was a good hunter. It followed slow-moving or injured plant-eating dinosaurs. It waited for the right time to attack. Tyrannosaurus rex used its sharp teeth to kill its prey.

The End of Tyrannosaurus Rex

Tyrannosaurus rex and other dinosaurs disappeared from Earth about 65 million years ago. Scientists are not sure why dinosaurs became extinct. Many scientists continue to study fossils to find out why the dinosaurs died out.

extinct
no longer living anywhere in the world

Alberta

Saskatchewan

CANADA

Montana

North Dakota

South Dakota

Wyoming

UNITED STATES

Utah

Colorado

New Mexico

Texas

Areas where Tyrannosaurus rex fossils have been found

Discovering Tyrannosaurus Rex

In 1900 and 1902, Barnum Brown discovered Tyrannosaurus rex fossils in Wyoming and Montana. Henry Fairfield Osborn named the fossils Tyrannosaurus rex in 1905. In 1990, a nearly complete Tyrannosaurus rex skeleton was dug up in South Dakota.

Studying Tyrannosaurus Rex Today

Paleontologists continue to study Tyrannosaurus rex fossils. Some paleontologists think Tyrannosaurus rex did not hunt for its own food. They think Tyrannosaurus rex was a scavenger that ate the meat other dinosaurs left behind.

paleontologist
a scientist who finds and studies fossils

Hands On: A Dinosaur Dig

Paleontologists dig for dinosaur fossils in the ground. Dinosaur skeletons usually are not complete. Paleontologists must remember where they found each bone. Paleontologists try to put the skeletons back together. This activity will show you how a paleontologist digs for fossils.

What You Need

A large flat container
Sand
Rocks, shells, twigs
Masking tape
Tweezers, toothpicks, spoons, or small shovels
Pencil
Paper
Index cards

What You Do

1. Fill the container with sand. Bury the rocks, shells, or twigs.
2. Divide the container into squares using the masking tape. Label each square with an index card.
3. Search for the items you buried. Carefully dig through the sand with the shovel. When you find an item use tweezers and toothpicks to remove it. Be careful not to break it.
4. Write down where you find each item.

Words to Know

dinosaur (DYE-na-sore)—an extinct land reptile; dinosaurs lived on Earth for more than 150 million years.

fossil (FOSS-uhl)—the remains or traces of something that once lived; bones and footprints can be fossils.

paleontologist (PAY-lee-on-TOL-ah-jist)—a scientist who finds and studies fossils

plain (PLANE)—a large, flat area of land

reptile (REP-tile)—a cold-blooded animal with a backbone; scales cover a reptile's body.

scientist (SYE-uhn-tist)—a person who studies the world around us

Read More

Landau, Elaine. *Tyrannosaurus Rex*. A True Book. New York: Children's Press, 1999.

Maynard, Christopher. *The Best Book of Dinosaurs*. New York: Kingfisher, 1998.

Rodriguez, K. S. *Tyrannosaurus Rex*. Prehistoric Creatures Then and Now. Austin, Texas: Raintree Steck-Vaughn, 2000.

Internet Sites

Sue at The Field Museum
http://www.fmnh.org/sue/
Tyrannosaurus Rex
http://www.zoomdinosaurs.com/subjects/dinosaurs/dinos/Trex.shtml
University of Wyoming Geological Museum Tour
http://www.uwyo.edu/geomuseum/Tour.htm

Index

DISCOVERING DINOSAURS

Capstone Press

Titles in this series:

Allosaurus
Ankylosaurus
Apatosaurus
Brachiosaurus
Diplodocus
Ichthyosaurus

Iguanodon
Pteranodon
Stegosaurus
Triceratops
Tyrannosaurus Rex
Velociraptor

Capstone press

http://www.capstonepress.com

ISBN 0-7368-3462-1

9 780736 834629

90000